An inter

Jenny Nimmo

EGMONT

Other authors in the series:

Enid Blyton, Theresa Breslin,
Gillian Cross, Anne Fine, Jamila Gavin,
Michelle Magorian, Michael Morpurgo,
Jacqueline Wilson

Wendy Cooling has been immersed in children's books since the start of her career. As a teacher she was responsible for running libraries, bookshops and help sessions for parents. She went on to run the Children's Book Foundation, and is now a consultant, book reviewer and in-service trainer for teachers and librarians. As well as editing story collections, Wendy organises the annual children's festival, Wordplay, and is on the judging panel for two major children's book awards.

First published in Great Britain 1999 by Mammoth Books Limited,
This edition published 2003 by Egmont Books Limited,
239 Kensington High Street, London W8 6SA.

Interview questions, design and typesetting © 1999 Egmont Books Limited
Interview answers © 1999 Jenny Nimmo
Jenny's Books © 1999 Wendy Cooling
Extract from *The Time Twister* © 2003 Jenny Nimmo

ISBN 1 4052 0411 7

10 9 8 7 6 5 4 3 2 1

A CIP catalogue record for this title is available from the British Library.

Printed and bound in Great Britain.

Contents

Foreword

Over a long career, Jenny Nimmo has written more than forty books for children, won the Smarties prize twice and been shortlisted for the Carnegie award three times. Many of her books, including *The Snow Spider* trilogy, have been adapted for stage and screen. And many reflect her experience of living in Wales, a land of legends, which she finds a very inspiring place.

Since she was originally interviewed in 1999, Jenny has written the mysterious and thrilling *Milo's Wolves*, inspired by the latest research into cloning. It was critically acclaimed and has been selected as a guided read for classes as an exemplar of work. She has also embarked on the *Children of the Red King* quintet, completing the first two volumes, *Midnight for Charlie*

Bone and *The Time Twister*. As the popularity of *Midnight for Charlie Bone* grows and grows, Jenny finds herself giving readings as far away as Florida to children hungry to hear more about Charlie Bone. And they won't be disappointed. Charlie's adventures at Bloor's continue in the sequel, *The Time Twister*, and Jenny already has the third volume underway.

Before now, Jenny's books such as *Griffin's Castle* and *The Rinaldi Ring* have been born out of situations where darkness and claustrophobia haunt characters and their families. Gwyn in *The Snow Spider*, like Charlie, also has magical gifts, but *The Snow Spider* trilogy highlights the burden of those gifts. Charlie Bone and the other endowed children are different. While Charlie has his own troubles to bear, he is also liberated by the battle between good and evil and the quest that he's drawn into. Far from trapping Charlie inside himself with depression, in *Children of the Red King* Jenny brings her characters out to fight this fundamental mythic battle, while also showing how the struggle can help them cope with everyday problems too. Jenny's infectious sense of humour, perhaps masked in her earlier work, is allowed to blossom vigorously in

Charlie's adventures.

As well as an author tour in America, the new series has brought Jenny, always greatly appreciated by some, the recognition of the many she has long deserved. Great praise poured from booksellers, adult reviewers and child readers alike. It's hard to imagine a more difficult audience than a thirteen-year-old boy, but just that audience responded instantly to *Midnight for Charlie Bone*, saying, 'Possibly the best book I have ever read . . . When I had finished the book, I went straight back to the beginning.' We can enjoy *Midnight for Charlie Bone* and *The Time Twister* for now, happily knowing there are still three more books in the quintet, and lots of Jenny's rich imagination, to look forward to.

Jenny Nimmo's (b.1944) enchanting children's books have been widely adapted for television and stage. Her books The Snow Spider *and* The Owl Tree *both won the Smarties Prize, and* Griffin's Castle *and* The Stone Mouse *were shortlisted for the Carnegie Medal.*

An interview with

Jenny Nimmo

by Wendy Cooling

I visited Jenny Nimmo at Henllan Mill in Wales and talked to her about her life and writing.

*   *   *

My family and my childhood

What was your family like?

There were really only two of us – my mother and myself – as my father died when I was five. My father's mother died when he was two, his father when he was eight, so I had no contact with them. I had a wonderful grandfather on my mother's side who had been in the army and trained horses – he was great fun. Granny was lovely too; they were both partly Irish and very warm. They lived in London so we didn't see much of them but we always saw them at Christmas.

I remember when my father was alive he used to buy me a book almost every Saturday; I really looked forward to it and that's probably where my love of books and stories started. *Babar the Elephant* was a terrific favourite and the Beatrix Potter books. *Rupert Bear* too.

My mum used to read to me every night; she was a good reader, a bit of an actress I suppose, as she put on funny voices. But I was sent away to school when I was six because she became very ill soon after my father died.

My childhood was really quite lonely. We lived on a farm, my uncle's farm, and I loved animals. I used to bring in stray cats and things but they were always taken from me – now I can keep them.

Where were you born?

I was born in Windsor but we moved to the borders

Jenny, aged a few weeks, with her mother.

between Berkshire and Surrey, to Chobham, where we lived until I was about seven.

What was your house like?

Jenny's father.

It was a lovely house called Founders and we were the first people to live in it as my father had had it built. He bought the land from my uncle who had a free-range chicken farm and I looked out of the window at acres and acres of chickens. There were rabbits and a cow called Trinket; her daughter was called Ruby and her granddaughter Jewel – three generations of Jersey cows. We grew our own vegetables and I think we were almost self-sufficient.

What was the nearest town?

Sunningdale was the nearest shopping centre. It had a level-crossing and I always used to imagine someone, or us, getting trapped between the gates. I remember an oak-beamed café where a Scottish family, the Beaties, made delicious scones.

Did you have a happy childhood?

It was a bit mixed. My uncle and aunt moved in when my father died. My uncle was the most wonderful person and a great influence in my life. He'd been a pilot before he bought the farm, but he'd fallen out of an aeroplane and injured his back. He wasn't wheelchair-bound but most of the time he had to lie flat on a wheeled wicker bed. He could get up though. He taught me to read with a book called *The Bear That Never Was*. My guardian used to buy me books too. He was a doctor and very tall. He made me feel safe. I adored him and called him Gentle Giant, or G.G.

Jenny's guardian (Dr Connell, or G.G.) and his wife.

What is your best childhood memory?

I seem to have more awful childhood memories than good ones. My mother sold our house when I was seven and we never had a real home again. I was always happy to go and see my grandparents. I remember the traditional Christmas celebrations – the tree was never decorated until Christmas Eve, and my grandfather would be up all night decorating it so that when we came down in the morning, there it was. They had a large family and I was probably very spoilt being the eldest grandchild and a sort of orphan.

What made you sad?

There were many sad days after my father died; my mother became ill and the house seemed to be in darkness. I wasn't allowed to have friends in and there seemed to be a great hole in my life. I remember my aunt making me stay in because I wouldn't make up my mind about going to the carnival. I was put in my room and started to cry, then my uncle struggled up the stairs and called, 'Robin' to me. I was always called Robin, I think because I used to wear a red jumper and hop! I was so amazed that he'd climbed the stairs. To cheer me up he gave me this beautiful silver inkstand; it was French and very old and I remember him telling me to put it by my bed. When my aunt saw it she was furious and said it was all a terrible mistake and I couldn't keep it.

Loneliness sometimes made me feel sad.

What were your first words?

No one ever said, but I'm told I talked in chunks. My mother said that my first phrase was, 'Give it to me, Angus, dear!' I'd obviously copied what I'd heard but I don't know how old I was.

*　　*　　*

My schooldays

What was your first school like?

My very first school was a little school a couple of miles from home. Very young children travelled there by themselves; they were given a penny for the bus and were put off at the right place.

I went away to boarding school when I was six and that's the school I remember most vividly. It was a mixed school in Kent for children of five to eleven.

Jenny aged six.

Most of the children had parents who lived abroad. They were either in the army or the diplomatic service.

My first day there was the most awful day in my childhood. I couldn't say a word, even when a boy punched me in the stomach. There was masses of room to play but no one on duty. I suppose one just learned to get by. The big dormitory was terrifying; there was one girl of about ten and the rest of us were much younger.

The school was really strict but I think, looking back, it was incredibly good academically because I was top in everything at the next school I went to when I was nine. I never achieved that again. In the first school, we really worked hard halfway through the night and I can't remember any fun there at all – apart from what we created for ourselves after lights out. My guardian used to take me out sometimes at weekends, and we were taken to the cinema about once a term.

Who was your favourite teacher?

At that school, a Polish music professor; the rest were all horrendous! The Principal's daughter was kind though. Her name was Sarah. We were often sent to bed with soaking wet hair, but once Sarah came round and took about three of us up to her room where she had a gas fire; she made us cocoa and dried our hair.

Did you wear uniform?

Jenny, aged nine, in her new school uniform.

The school uniform was incredibly ugly – grey belted tunics that made us look like sacks of potatoes and purple hats a bit like Salvation Army bonnets.

What was your secondary school like?

Much more fun and everyone was happy. They were keen on music, drama, dancing and art.

What was your favourite subject?

History; I loved all those stories about kings and queens and people losing their heads, battles and castles – I liked the fact that it was all true. My history teacher was very good but strict

Jenny (right), aged eleven, with school friends.

– not above rapping your knuckles or throwing things. I fell in love with Charles II; he had a great face and his life seemed very romantic. I didn't like science very much, probably because I didn't like the teacher. I was supposed to enjoy it because my father had been a physicist.

Was reading important to you?

I was extremely naughty as I got older and used to like making people laugh and sending up the teachers. I always wanted to read, though, and introduced myself to books. I remember I'd gone through all the books in the junior library by the time I was nine and a half and asked permission to go into the senior one – you weren't allowed in there until you were eleven. I pleaded, and the inscrutable English teacher who used to wear the key round her neck, unlocked it and let me in. I remember her putting the key in the lock to this wonderful treasure chest and then writing down the book I borrowed – the first one I took was *Gone With the Wind*. I adored the book and couldn't be dragged away from it. After that, she would just open up the library and tell me to help myself; I read everything and especially loved biographies.

Was writing important to you?

English was my best subject. I loved writing; they would give us a subject and I liked to veer off course – when the subject was wheels, I remember writing about the chariot that dragged dead Hector round the walls of Troy. There was nearly always a dead body in my stories.

Words meant a lot. I used to tell stories and got into

Jenny (centre, top, wearing a round hat) in a school play.

trouble for entertaining the dorm with creepy stories; I always did the sound effects like doors opening and thundering hooves. I liked to make newspapers and write plays and put them on.

Did the teachers encourage you with your writing?

They were keen for me to go into the theatre; I think because the famous actress Jill Bennett had gone to the school and they fancied nurturing another actress. They didn't encourage me to write.

Were friends important as you grew older?

I had a large group of friends as I got older but was quite

reserved – I needed space as well as people.

What was your favourite children's book?

My favourite book when I was eight was *The Lion, the Witch and the Wardrobe* and I still love it; I've never got over the magic of the moment when Lucy steps through the back of the wardrobe into the snow. I enjoyed sharing *Where the Wild Things Are* with all my children; we all loved the magic, the language and the brilliance of it.

Were you interested in sport?

I liked hockey, especially because you got to go out if you were in the team, and I was long-jump champion three years running. I don't participate in sport now but I love to watch rugby, it's a very Welsh thing. It's rough but I enjoy the excitement of it and the rest of the family love it. We even named our cat Neil Jenkins after the brilliant Welsh fly-half.

What about music?

I always loved music and played the piano until I left

school and my mother gave the piano away. I like Mozart for relaxation and film music to stimulate me when I'm writing. It can inspire dramatic or nostalgic scenes. I never got into pop music, much to my children's disgust. I wasn't aware of it at school where it was just classical music and choir practices. My favourite music is Mozart's *Requiem* and I remember crying through his biography.

And art?

In Chobham, we lived opposite a man who I was told was a very famous artist so I always revered artists.

I loved drawing but don't mention it now because my husband is a professional painter. All my children are wonderful artists; their work gives me tremendous pleasure. I like abstract art and would love to own a Matisse.

Were films important in your life?

I didn't often go to the cinema but when I was very small was taken by a nanny illicitly to see *Jane Eyre* and *Rebecca* – I think she was meeting her boyfriend there. I remember certain images – Rochester on a white horse and the mad boy running on a beach. I went to the theatre with my mother in the holidays and, as my guardian was married to Dame Ninette de Valois, I used to get tickets for the ballet. Gregory Peck was a film star I liked and later Laurence Olivier.

As a child, my favourite film was *Bambi*, now it's the French film, *Jules et Jim*.

Do you watch television?

I watch *The Late Review* on TV – if you are widely at odds with public opinion, it's reassuring to listen to people you admire whose opinions are widely at odds with each other.

* * *

My career

What did you do when you left school?

I left school when I was sixteen and went into the theatre. The adults wanted me to go to university, but I'd had enough of educational establishments. I'd been

Jenny, aged sixteen, as Gwendolin in 'The Importance of Being Ernest'.

to the local rep theatre near Bexhill and I was determined to get into the theatre; my mother was horrified and I had to go on hunger strike or something before I was allowed to enter the theatre as a student. It changed my life. Actors can be egocentric but they are warm, compassionate and funny. They saved me. It was wonderful – I made the tea, often put the wrong props on the stage, stayed till midnight and every now and then got to play a part. Slowly I moved on to be an Assistant Stage Manager and finally Juvenile Lead.

What did you do next?

I couldn't get theatre work in London but I was desperate to get there so, when I was in my early twenties, I went to the BBC. I had no qualifications except acting experience and seven reasonable O levels. As I was leaving the interviewer asked me if I liked music and I said 'Yes'. He offered me a job in music copyright and soon I had my own office. After a while I became rather fed up with the work and went to Italy to look after three Italian boys. When I returned I got a job as a photographic researcher in TV. One day I saw an old theatre friend who persuaded me to become an Assistant Floor Manager. I started on the News at Alexandra Palace. It was before the days of robot cameras so the Floor Manager was the newcaster's only link with the gallery – feeding stories in, making sure he was happy – it was live and it was exciting.

Then I moved to light entertainment shows and *Jackanory*; that's where I came into contact with children's fiction. An Irish director said, 'Why don't you write your own story, Jenny, and start directing?' I applied for the job and before I knew it I was directing. It was quite frightening. Anna Home was my producer and halfway through a recording she suddenly left me to it. It was she who read my story, *The Bronze Trumpeter*, and told me it was good. It was my first book. I met Ray Smith, a Welsh actor who introduced me to Wales and the legends in *The Mabinogion*. Around the same time I went to a party with two girl friends and met David, now my husband, who was also talking about Welsh legends. I was suddenly engulfed in Welshness and that's why I'm in Wales now. David introduced me to his agents, Gina and Murray Pollinger, who helped to get *The Bronze Trumpeter* published and we moved to Wales. Writing was rather on hold for about ten years as I had three children. When the youngest started nursery school, I got going again and *Tatty Apple* was my new beginning.

*   *   *

My career as a writer

Did you write as a child?

I wrote masses of plays when I was a child and a story about a man who murdered a train driver because the train had crashed and his wife had died. That story was thrown back at me by the teacher who didn't think I should have been writing about murders.

When did you decide to become a professional writer?

I became a writer because of my time on *Jackanory* and because I could write at home. I was heart-broken when *Jackanory* finished; children loved it and nothing offers that storytelling now. My writing got going seriously when I moved to Wales. I was encouraged by Anna Home from the BBC and by the actor, Ray Smith – he was the influence behind *The Snow Spider*.

Who inspired you?

I was inspired by the writer, Bruce Chatwin; his book *On the Black Hill* changed everything about the way I was writing and thinking. That book seemed to turn my writing round, Chatwin's language has a wonderful rhythm to it that is perfect to read aloud.

Do you like being a writer?

I do like being a writer but sometimes when the

deadlines and the pressure are daunting I wonder why. It's hard because I can never afford to do just one book at a time; I need two or three on the go to survive. It's quite a lonely job but I don't mind – sometimes other people don't understand my need to carry on and the impossibility of stopping for a cup of tea. It's sometimes very hard, especially writing a picture book text – a long book is a luxury. I hope my books are easier to read aloud now that my style has developed.

Is there anything you have to do before you start writing?

Before I start writing I need to know that everyone's fed – it used to be the children and now it's the chickens and the cats and rabbits. I have to have blue pencils to write with, 3B, and they're becoming very difficult to find.

Is there a pattern to the writing day?

There's no real pattern to my work. I sit down in the morning and in the next twelve hours sometimes I just do a paragraph and sometimes twenty pages. I write over and over and my bin is full of paper after about half an hour. I can hardly write a sentence without changing it, then I edit – rewriting every line, every word, every paragraph, every chapter.

Do you let anyone read your manuscript before you send it off?

My elder daughter Myfanwy used to read my books but it was harder for the other two who are dyslexic; I think they're probably all kind about them. My husband David reads my manuscripts and then they go to the editor – typed by this time on my computer. I'm lucky with my editors and do more work in response to their comments; they know best for by this time I can't be objective any more, I'm just too involved.

Where do you get your ideas?

Ideas come from everywhere – newspapers, eavesdropping, magazines, TV can all trigger something.

Why do you write for children?

Probably because it all started when I was working on a children's programme, it seemed the natural thing to do. I thought I might write for adults when my youngest child left home but seem to be writing for younger children instead. I used to tell my children stories but the eldest became so good that she took over.

Do you do lots of research?

I do an enormous amount of research sometimes but only a fraction is apparent in a book. For *Ultramarine* I had to find out exactly how to treat oiled birds, so I went to the RSPB and got masses of data on how many oiled birds were found, how many died and what to do. I had to get it right in the book in case a child ever found an oiled bird. *The Rinaldi Ring* took three years to complete because of all the research. I read a great many books about World War I, both fiction and non-fiction; I had to know what it felt like to be bereaved in the War. The idea for the book came from my younger daughter, Gwenhwyfar, who suggested a story about a ghost and a ring. Other books are inspired by the countryside.

How important is the imagination?

I think the imagination is everything; it's wonderful as

it sets you free; always in a book there's that moment when the imagination takes over and off you go, the sky's the limit. Sometimes stories begin with real situations but after that I take off into the unknown.

Do you base your characters on real people?

Nain in *The Snow Spider* was suggested by my children's music teacher – her hen used to sleep in a chair and so parents waiting for their children to come down from a lesson had to be careful where they sat. I've used facets of my children's and their friends' personalities; bits of people – I almost got matron from my boarding school into my book, *Toby in the Dark*. It became so like her and I was so frightened of her that I went over the top and had to be pulled back by my editor.

What matters most to you – the story or the characters?

Story and characters are of equal importance – the characters make the story but having the characters without the story would be pointless.

How has your real life affected your stories?

Although I wrote a great deal before I had children of my own, they've changed the way I write, made me move from the way I thought as a child and have given me a broader view.

I've only realised later how my own life has touched my writing. My life as a child is very tied up with *Griffin's Castle* but I was unconscious of it at the time. Writing about a girl who wanted a place of her own made me suddenly realise that that was what I had wanted. People say that I'm always writing about someone who's lost a parent and it's true that I find it hard to write about a family with two parents.

Wales has influenced me a lot for, coming to it as a stranger, I was really struck by everything in the landscape. I somehow wanted to get it all down, to catch it before it was lost, but of course it's going to be there forever. The way you see it changes but that first impression is so stunning, you see things that people who've lived here all their lives might not. I wanted to get it all into *The Snow Spider*. I always like to know the environment where my characters live.

Which of your books do you like best?

The Snow Spider is my most successful book. I put so much into it; I wanted to get everything in – Hallowe'en, people disappearing, magic, mountains, other worlds – I crammed it all in and it seemed to work. I became very fond of Dinah in *Griffin's Castle* because she was the sort of person I wanted to be – tough and brave – but never was. (My husband disagrees. He says I'm very like her.) She's certainly the character I empathise most with. I was quite upset when a reviewer didn't like her.

Are pictures and covers important to you?

Living in a family of artists, pictures and covers matter a lot. We all get covers we don't like and covers we do. I've been really lucky with the illustrators I've been given.

What gives you most satisfaction about being a writer?

It's great when something just works. Talking to

children is very important because they're honest; meeting children who've believed in your book and enjoyed it is very satisfying. Children think of things I haven't – one recently wanted to know what the baby in *The Owl Tree* was called and I just didn't know. This prompted an interesting discussion.

Is there anything you dislike about being a writer?

Not really, though I probably take too much notice of reviews; a bad one can be devastating. Writing is probably the nicest thing you could ever do; you can reach out and communicate but don't have the terrible disadvantage of being recognised in the street.

What do you hope to achieve with your books?

I don't think much about what I want to achieve – I just want children to enjoy my books – and it would be nice if they were buying them too!

Why do you think fiction is important?

Of all the things that opened my mind, books are special; they give you experiences, they're friends and there's an endless supply – the world's your oyster! You can be anywhere, in any situation, and books offer connections. I read that when the journalist John McCarthy was a hostage in Beirut, a bedraggled friend, Brian Keenan, was thrown into the same cell and McCarthy wryly remarked: 'My God, it's Ben Gunn!' – there really are some books and some characters that we all know. Books can unite people and cross languages and stories are important the world over.

Fiction might be even stronger in the new century as people turn away from things that don't really satisfy them as much as books. We need stories but I'm not against TV; it can introduce good fiction.

Are there any books that have influenced your life?

On the Black Hill, by Bruce Chatwin, that I've already mentioned, is the book that has influenced me most. It's the story of Welsh twins, not exciting on the face of it but the adventure is their lives and communication and love for each other, and their feeling for the countryside and their farm. It's beautifully written, set in the mountains between England and Wales. Most important is the language Bruce Chatwin uses, the images – somehow the language, the atmosphere and the characters come together to make a perfect whole.

What are your top ten books?

There's no ranking here as the books are chosen for different reasons:

Babar the Elephant (Laurence de Brunhoff) because he was my childhood and I still have an ancient copy with my untidy scribbles in it.

The Children of the New Forest (Captain Frederick Marryat) was probably the first history-based book I read. I was engrossed in the story of the children's survival after their house is burnt down and their parents vanish.

Where the Wild Things Are (Maurice Sendak) because my children loved it.

The Haunting (Margaret Mahy) which I enjoyed as much as they did.

The Iron Man (Ted Hughes) because of the language and because it's frightening and different, quite unique. It's my son's favourite book.

The Snowman (Raymond Briggs) – we went back to it over and over again for comfort.

Goblin Market (Christina Rossetti) and *The Lady of Shalott* (Alfred, Lord Tennyson) for their wonderful language and powerful imagery.

Captain Charteris - Jenny's Uncle Ronnie who taught her to read.

The Lion, the Witch and the Wardrobe (C.S. Lewis) because I loved it and my eldest daughter used to say, 'I wish I could live in Narnia' whenever things were difficult.

On the Black Hill (Bruce Chatwin) because it really changed my approach to writing.

Jenny's Books
An overview by Wendy Cooling

The Bronze Trumpeter

Jenny Nimmo's first book, *The Bronze Trumpeter*, was published in 1974, just a quarter of a century ago. It tells the story of an only child, a rich but very lonely boy, living in a kind of silence in a grand villa in Sicily. The book is an early indicator of Jenny Nimmo's boundless imagination and powerful language, and, like many of her later books, it reflects the loneliness of her own childhood.

Paolo's father, the Count di Montorella, is away fighting in World War I and his mother has withdrawn into sadness and seldom leaves her room. Paolo is left in the care of servants who are forbidden to talk to him, and a wicked stepmother-like character, the governess Fraulein Helga. She is a terrifying figure, her 'small eyes were the colour of dull steel' and her 'stiff dresses were wrapped so tightly round her that she creaked as she walked', and she ruled Paolo with relentless discipline. During one of his rare moments of freedom he discovers a wild area of garden that he has never seen before and in it he finds the Bronze Trumpeter, a boy who stands in the centre of a pond, his trumpet raised to his lips. He acts as a fountain and water cascades from his trumpet into the pond below. The meeting between boy and trumpeter marks a change in Paolo's life and his mind opens to the magic and fantasy that unfolds as the story is told.

The characters involved in Paolo's day-to-day life – governess, gardener and maid – are finely drawn but his mother remains a shadow, open to the reader's condemnation for her selfish neglect of her son who misses his father just as she does. In spite of the timeless, changeless feeling of the story's opening, something is always happening and the pace of the story really accelerates with the arrival in the village of three painted wagons carrying Harlequin and a troop of actors. Paolo's involvement in their project – to put on a play in the theatre that lies hidden in the villa's overgrown gardens, a theatre that has not been seen for over a century – leads him through his loneliness into experiences that strengthen and excite him. The story is of adventure, struggle, danger and magic. Paolo knows that he has experienced something rare and extraordinary, something only on offer to those who are sensitive and needy, something that will change him forever.

The Bronze Trumpeter is a powerful first novel, the only one of Jenny's books written in her pre-Wales years. It has the magic and fantasy that has become associated with her writing, as well as a strong sense of place. The wild, endless, sometimes claustrophobic gardens of the Villa Montorella trap the characters and the reader in a world that can't really be understood. The question in the reader's mind as the last page is read is, 'Where does reality end and fantasy begin?' – it is a question raised over and over again by Jenny's stories.

Tatty Apple

Jenny moved to Wales in 1974 and writing took a back seat as her three children grew up. *Tatty Apple*, her first book for younger children, came in 1984 and was dedicated to Myfanwy, Ianto and Gwenhwyfar, her own children. It is an exuberant story, full of magic and wonder and more than a touch of humour. Again the family at the centre of the story is mourning the loss of a father and Owen-Owen, the oldest child, is missing him a lot. O-O, as his sister calls him, had been promised a trip with his father on the little local train that travels down the valley to Welshpool and is sad that the shared journey will never take place. As Owen-Owen is fetching a red hen for his sister to bribe her to go with him on the train, he finds Tatty Apple, a green rabbit. He scoops up the rabbit and carries him home and life is never quite the same again.

The story is set in mid-Wales; the little train actually runs behind the converted water mill that is Jenny's home.

Everything in Owen-Owen's land was green; trees, meadows, hedges, the winding river and the mossy stones beside it. Even the slate roofs in the village were green with lichen; everything was green except the Engine, and that was as red as a poppy. So, living, as he did, in this green land, Owen should not have been surprised when he saw a green rabbit.

The green rabbit soon shows a talent for magic; magic that almost runs out of control. But the magic is powerful and Tatty Apple is always able to help when the family is in trouble.

The village where everyone knows everyone is very real; the dialogue is full of the rhythms of Wales and the fast-moving story has almost more magic than can be contained. There's warmth and humour, too, in this tale that perfectly mixes reality and fantasy and really speaks to young readers.

The Snow Spider Trilogy

Jenny is probably best known for this wonderful trilogy, again set in the Wales she knows so well, but this time influenced by *The Mabinogion*, so often at the heart of Welsh Literature. Reading *The Mabinogion*, a collection of old stories – myths, romances, tales of great heroes, Arthurian stories and more – was one of the ingredients that came together in her life and resulted in her falling under a sort of Welsh spell.

The Snow Spider won the Smarties Grand Prix and the Tir na n'Og – an award given by the Welsh Arts Council. All three stories in the trilogy reached huge audiences when they were adapted and serialised for TV.

The Snow Spider is a gripping fantasy; it's mystical and lyrical and really marks a turning point in Jenny's writing for it is told in wonderfully rhythmic language that makes it perfect to read aloud. There are again echoes of the writer's life – her son Ianto was interested in the stars when she was working on the book, and her daughter Gwenhwyfar kept spiders in her dolls' house! Nia, the central character in *Emlyn's Moon*, the second book in the triology, has difficulty at school and two of Jenny's children had to fight with dyslexia and all the problems involved. Gwen, like Nia in the story, won a prize for collage at the local Eisteddfod.

These books are packed with mystery, magic and happenings. Again Jenny Nimmo weaves together real life and fantasy. In *The Snow Spider*, Gwyn is told by his grandmother that he is a magician as she gives him five presents on his ninth birthday. The piece of seaweed, yellow scarf, tin whistle, twisted metal brooch and small, broken horse seem strange presents, but they all have a part to play in Gwyn's extraordinary quest; a quest tied up with the past and with his sister's unexplained disappearance. As he moves through dangers that the magician in him demands, Gwyn must also cope with painful feelings of confusion, loss and rejection – as well as the usual problems of family and school life and the ups and downs of friendships. The healing of the family is another important element in the story. The characters are strongly established and firmly placed in rural Wales where the environment, and the weather, are permanent influences on people's lives. Our sympathy is with Gwyn as he struggles to complete a task that he can hardly comprehend and yet it is Nain, his wonderfully eccentric grandmother, who remains in our minds long after the book is finished.

Emlyn's Moon is peopled with many of the characters from *The Snow Spider*, but this time Nia, a daughter of Gwyn's neighbours, is the central character. She is sensitively drawn, a young girl who feels a huge sense of inadequacy, and again the problems of her real life are mixed with magic as the story unfolds. Gwyn's magic has an important part to play, but it is the realness of the world in which the story is set that makes us take the story seriously and celebrate Nia's victory.

Gwyn is thirteen when the final book in the trilogy, *The Chestnut Soldier*, begins. Although this book is a love story, Gwyn's magic is still important, this time centring on the evil influence of the broken horse he has had since his ninth birthday. This will be his final challenge and he hopes that his magic powers will disappear and let him move on to just being ordinary. The evil of the broken horse, a more dark and dangerous magic that Gwyn cannot control, moves into Evan Llyr, a soldier staying with Nia's family to recuperate after being injured in Northern Ireland. This time, although Gwyn and Nia have important parts to play, it is Nia's sixteen-year-old sister, Catrin, who gets caught up in the spell and must find a way through to a calmer life.

These three books offers a wonderful reading experience and show Jenny Nimmo as a real master of fantasy writing; as a writer able to blend reality and fantasy into stories that hold readers to the end and leave them wanting more. The strength of the characters, the action-packed plots and the rhythm of the language combine to make stories that have a timeless quality.

Ultramarine *and* Rainbow and Mr Zed

These two novels for readers of ten years plus

move away from the familiar Welsh village to a sea setting. The environment is even more important; the imagery and power of the sea is in fact central in both books. The lives of Ned and Nell are dominated by the sea and a theme of conservation, of saving the sea and its creatures from thoughtless exploitation, is explored. Again the plots are complex as the mystery of the children's background slowly unravels and their affinity for the sea is explained. The element of fantasy is strong as mysterious characters enter the story, but there is reality too as the children work to save oil-damaged birds and at the same time become aware that there is something very unusual about their family and their past.

Ned and Nell are drawn into situations that test them. This time the grandmother who suddenly appears to look after them is frightening and evil as she brings danger into their lives, but the power of the man who comes in from the sea overcomes the evil. The quality of writing draws the reader into this strange and magical family and makes the confrontation between Nell, her father and her uncle, Mr Zed, in the second book, dramatic and memorable. Mr Zed wants to own the power and the riches of the sea and use them for his own purposes; Nell and her father are determined to restore things to a natural state. Wonderful seascapes and magical, colourful characters offer the perfect setting for the exploration of this still topical conservation theme. But although the writer invites readers to think about an important issue, it is the power of the stories, the setting and the characterisations that are at the heart of these splendid books.

Shorter novels

Jenny Nimmo writes with confidence for younger children and shorter novels by her have appeared every year since 1989. They show the richness of her imagination and her range as a storyteller. There are too many to mention here but some are just too good to be missed. *Delilah and the Dogspell* is the first of three books about Delilah, a fiercely wonderful cat; a cat with 'eyes as yellow as dandelions and fur like wild smoke, all grey and curling' and whiskers that are 'long and silvery' and 'an unusual turned-up nose'. When first introduced, Delilah is 'sitting on a red velvet cushion' wearing 'a collar studded with sparkling crystals'. She is indeed a queen among cats and she has powerful magic – she can shrink dogs! The three Delilah stories are perfect for readers of seven to ten; they're packed with humour, adventure and magic and were hugely successful when read on *Jackanory*. Jenny really lets her sense of fun run riot in these totally satisfying stories.

Wilfred's Wolf is a very original, almost mythical story, that tells of Wolf's journey from the dark Arctic forests to The Plush, the poshest hotel in London where, with the help of the head chef, Wilfred, a lover of wolves, he learns to cook. The story is full of fun. It is an adventure and a love story with a happy ending; it's an unlikely story but Jenny Nimmo tells it with such style that it is one of those special tales that can be enjoyed by readers of all ages. The humour in *The Bears Will Get You!* has the same appeal – at least to anyone who has ever tried to avoid the cracks in the pavement.

Series titles, too, don't disappoint. *Alien on the 99th Floor* is a very popular Banana Book with its fast-moving mix of alien adventure, humour and a shopping trip that turns out to be more fun than expected. *Granny Grimm's Gruesome Glasses* in the Jets series is told in a mix of speech bubbles and text and is a wonderful joke as Fiona Smiley and Granny Grimm change places. Granny rather enjoys her new life but Fiona is not at all keen. However, the experience is not wasted and Fiona learns a lot during her time as Granny Grimm and returns to her own life with skills that she had never imagined were possible.

The common element in all these stories is fantasy; however real Jenny Nimmo's worlds are, they are always touched by a little or a lot of magic. *The Dragon's Child* is magical in every way for we should know that there are no such things as dragons. Dando is the youngest of all the dragons and he still can't fly. This is a real worry for his mother as the dragons are ready to fly south in search of safer hands. Dando is left alone until an orphaned slave girl offers him hope and friendship that is strong enough to keep them both safe. This story has the quality of a myth and keeps alive the idea of dragons.

The two real gems among these shorter books are *The Stone Mouse* and *The Owl Tree*. Both books received critical acclaim and *The Owl Tree* won the Smarties Prize, a prize in which the final choices are made by young readers themselves. The texts are spare and take us into small, simple worlds which are created with perfection and style. *The Stone Mouse* is about a pebble left guarding Aunt Maria's house as the Martin family come to house-sit – it is a magical stone mouse or a 'dirty old pebble' depending on whether you are a sensitive little girl called Ellie, or her angry brother Ted. This is a gentle, sensitively-written story, highly original, at times funny and with the writer's usual strong sense of place. The seaside house with its tricky stove swiftly becomes a world for the story and the reader to inhabit.

The owl tree is huge and leafy and shivers with

fear as Joe sees it through his window. The tree is part of Granny Diamond's world but her neighbour wants to cut it down. Joe knows it has secrets to tell and that he must find the courage to save it. The owl tree is the symbol around which the events of the story take place and also the catalyst for Joe's growing-up and conquering of his own fear. Both books are highly atmospheric and written in simple but rhythmic language that makes them ideal to read aloud. The magic is gentle and good and the stories show imagination and eloquence working together perfectly.

Picture books

Writing texts for picture books is one of the most challenging tasks for a writer. The words are strictly limited and every one must play its part. Jenny has produced five picture books all with a very traditional feel. There are retellings of familiar stories – *Thumbelina* and a Cinderella that reaches back to Celtic roots in *The Starlight Cloak*. The latter was successfully adapted for the stage by the Polka Children's Theatre. Then came *The*

Witches and the Singing Mice, an original story with all the ingredients of a traditional tale. The tiny singing mice come under the spell of three witches who come to Glenmagraw, and fear spreads through the village as children are struck down with sleeping sickness. Only two brave cats can break the magic and bring safety back to the village. The intriguing story has a haunting quality complemented by Angela Barrett's fine illustrations – it is a wonder to read aloud.

Jenny's most recent picture books, produced in partnership with the brilliant Welsh artist, Jac Jones, return to the mythology of Wales. *Gwion and the Witch* is a well-loved Welsh legend and Jenny's version has all the humour, rhythm and drama that a good tale needs. The high point of the story is a fantastic shape-changing sequence in which Gwion battles to escape the witch – as he becomes a hare the witch becomes a hound, when he is a fish she becomes an otter, he becomes a bird and she becomes a hawk and the chase goes on until Gwion becomes a speck of grain and the witch, now a sleek red hen, eats him

– but that, of course, is not the end of the story!

Branwen, a very different story, sees Jenny returning again to *The Mabinogion* to retell one of the saddest stories ever told. It is a powerful story of kings and queens, love and jealousy, joy and pain and it touches the heart of every new reader. The texts of these picture books show the maturity and skill of the writer as the language flows and reads like poetry.

Griffin's Castle *and* The Rinaldi Ring

These two quite recent novels are for older readers of perhaps eleven or twelve plus. *Griffin's Castle* is a gripping, quite menacing fantasy with a marvellously strong and real central character. Dinah and her mother are always on the move and Dinah, rather like the young Jenny Nimmo, is desperate to have a permanent home, somewhere where she can really belong. When Gomer Gwynne lends them his ramshackle old empty house, Dinah dreams that it will be theirs forever. However, Gomer is interested only in her mother and represents a real threat to Dinah herself. Dinah conjures up the stone animals from the castle wall to protect her as she struggles to make the old house into a home. But she realises that she needs more than the house and the strange beasts, and looks into the past to find a possible way to happiness with her great-grandfather. *Griffin's Castle* is a terrific read as the author creates a powerful sense of atmosphere that makes the book impossible to put down. The tough, resilient Dinah is clever and strong; she inspires loyalty in those she meets and friends help her to cope with a life that at times offers little hope – she is perhaps Jenny's most convincing character.

The Rinaldi Ring is a brilliant story that moves from America to England, and from the present back to World War I. It is complex and challenging; an adventure, almost a thriller, but most of all a story that tells of the power of love and hate. Eliot returns to England with his father after his mother's death and is sent to live with relations he hardly knows. He immediately senses strange threats that he doesn't understand and the haunting begins. Eliot knows he must solve the mystery and right a terrible wrong if he is to have any peace. So much goes on in this book and only a skilled storyteller could weave together so many strands, bringing the story to a convincing and satisfactory conclusion. It is the work of a confident writer, a writer willing to take risks and is a book that can be enjoyed by all young adults.

Where next?

Jenny has written for young people of five to fifteen and has given us books of great variety. She has also contributed fine short stories to a number of anthologies. In 'Tree Talk', a young boy senses communication from trees and learns important things about his past; 'Take Your Knee Off My Heart' tells the wonderful story of a first kiss; 'The Winter Sister' is a heart-breaking story of loss and misunderstanding leading to more tragedy, and 'The Last Prince' returns to Welsh history to tell of princes and poets. These are all stories for mature readers but show something of the writer's range of genre. She has become a great drawer of characters and a powerful writer of fantasy and more; she knows how to use humour and atmosphere and to enclose her readers in a story. The future could bring anything, for there are surely many more wonderful stories to look forward to.

Wendy Cooling

1999

Bibliography

In date order

The Bronze Trumpeter

Angus and Robertson 1974; Mammoth 1996

Paolo is alone and friendless in the grand but cheerless Villa Montorello, his only companion a harsh governess. But Paolo does have one pleasure: hidden in the neglected garden is the Bronze Trumpeter, a magical statue. Then Paolo meets Harlequin and the 'Comedians' who have returned from the mists of time to bring joy and laughter to the village once more. But why is Paolo's governess so afraid of the Comedians?

Preis der Leiseratten, awarded by the Austrian Minister of Culture. Published in German as Nachmittag mit Harlekin *1982.*

Tatty Apple

Methuen 1984; Mammoth 1990

Owen-Owen discovers a strange green rabbit on the mountainside one day and takes him home. Tatty Apple turns out to be a magic rabbit, creating fun and mischief and ultimately saving Owen's family and neighbours from danger.

The Snow Spider

Methuen 1986 (hb); Mammoth 1990 (pb)

On his ninth birthday Gwyn is given some strange gifts by his grandmother. They lead him to the Snow Spider and a series of encounters with strange other worlds of snow and silver, finally revealing the fate of his lost elder sister.

Overall Winner of the Smarties Prize 1986.

Winner of the Tir na n'Og 1997.

Emlyn's Moon

Mammoth 1987

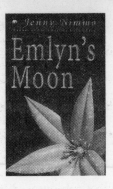

In this second book in the Snow Spider trilogy, Nia is warned against entering Llewelyn's chapel but does so, and there, with the help of Emlyn and his artist father, discovers a special gift which she was unaware she possessed. But when Emlyn is in danger, it is Gwyn, the boy magician, who must save him.

Published in the US as Orchard of the Crescent Moon *1989.*

The Chestnut Soldier

Methuen 1989 (hb); Mammoth 1990 (pb)

The last of the Snow Spider trilogy. Gwyn faces his greatest challenge when the enigmatic and charming Evan Llyr appears, inspiring Gwyn's pity but also forcing him to do battle, possibly to the death.

The Red Secret

Hamish Hamilton 1989

When Mr Turner becomes headmaster of Applefield Primary School his family move from the town to the country. The story tells of Tom and Daisy's struggle to cope with a very different life. It is a fox cub, Rufus, who makes a difference and begins to give Tom and Daisy a sense of belonging.

Jupiter Boots

Heinemann 1990

Timmy's shoes are too small but his mother has no time or money to buy him new ones. Then he finds the Jupiter Boots, which take him on a magical trip to the stars; but when he comes back down to Earth he knows they're not really his to keep.

Ultramarine

Methuen 1990 (hb); Mammoth 1992 (pb)

Ned and Nell learn about a girl called Ultramarine, who turns out to be the reason for their grandmother's hatred, not only of the sea and all its creatures, but also of them. Only Arion, a man from the sea, can help them.

The Bears Will Get You

Methuen 1990 (hb); Mammoth 1992 (pb)

Treading on the cracks in the pavement can be a dangerous thing to do if you don't believe there are any bears, as Simon, Alice and the others discover. But once they're in the Bears' living room under Spa Drive, how do they get back?

Delilah and the Dogspell

Methuen 1991 (hb); Mammoth 1992 (pb)

Delilah is a remarkable cat who specialises in dogspells, shrinking all those who dare to attack her. But things start to get out of hand, and Annie, who moves in next door, decides something must be done.

The Witches and the Singing Mice

Collins 1993

When children in the village of Glemagraw begin to fall under a spell, two brave cats set out to save them. The cats must break the power of three witches who have moved into the village determined to get their evil way. *Published in Germany as* Drei Hexen, drei Katzen und die singenden Mause. *Winner of the 1994 Rattenfanger Literaturpreis, awarded every two years by the city of Hameln.*

Rainbow and Mr Zed

Methuen 1992 (hb); Mammoth 1993 (pb)

The sequel to *Ultramarine*, this novel follows the adventures of Nell, who has to leave home to stay with relatives she barely knows. However, she soons meets a homesick ghost and a man named Mr Zed who owns an island which Nell realises she may never escape from.

The Starlight Cloak

Collins 1993

Oona lives a miserable life, working for her two spiteful

sisters, until one day her foster-mother conjures up a magical outfit of shimmering beauty and the way opens for her to find love and happiness. This unusual version of the Cinderella story is drawn from traditional Celtic roots.

Delilah and the Dishwasher Dogs

Methuen 1993 (hb); Mammoth 1996 (pb)

When Tabby Jack witnesses the arrival of two miniature dogs, there is only one thing the cat can do – fetch Delilah, whose knowledge of magic is a match for anyone.

The Stone Mouse

Walker 1994

When the Martin family come to stay at Aunt Maria's seaside cottage, they find the Stone Mouse waiting for them. Ellie is enchanted, but her brother Ted angrily dismisses it as a 'dirty old pebble'. Can the Stone Mouse win Ted over before it loses all its magical powers and goes back to being a simple grey pebble?

Shortlisted for the Carnegie Medal 1994

Griffin's Castle

Methuen 1994 (hb); Mammoth 1995 (hb)

When Gomer Gwynne lets Dinah and her mother live in his empty house, Dinah, who has never had a home, thinks that it will be forever. But, as Christmas approaches, she learns that Gomer intends to rob her of everything. A fierce determination grows within her, and when she sees the stone creatures on the castle wall, extraordinary things begin to happen.

Shortlisted for: Carnegie Medal 1995; Nottingham Children's Book Award 1995 Oak Tree Award; Smarties Book Prize 1994 9-11 category; Whitbread Award 1994 children's category; WH Smith's Mindboggling Books Award 1995.

The Breadwitch

Heinemann 1993

Peter gets special bread to help his little sister who doesn't like eating. But Belinda soon has a big appetite, and so do the birds and the cats in the garden where crumbs from the special bread have been thrown. Peter has to find his friend, the Breadwitch, to see if she will reverse the process.

Granny Grimm's Gruesome Glasses

HarperCollins 1995

A young girl thinks that wearing glasses will make her brainy like the rest of her family – so when she sees Granny Grimm's glasses lying on the garden wall she just can't resist trying them on!

Wilfred's Wolf

Red Fox 1995

Wolf journeys from the Arctic forests to The Plush, the poshest hotel in London where, with the help of head chef Wilfred, he learns to cook.

Ronnie and the Giant Millipede

Walker Books 1995

A little boy cannot stop the urge to stamp on everything in his new boots. His mother warns him that one day he may, like his ancestor, Rumpelstiltskin, stamp his way right through the floor.

The Witch's Tears

HarperCollins 1996

A stranger, Mrs Scarum, takes shelter in Theo's house during a terrible storm. She's full of magic and her tears turn to crystal as they fall. This story has a wonderful sense of atmosphere – and a happy ending, as Mrs Scarum gives Mrs Blossom a sparkling crystal necklace, as well as the safe return of her husband.

Alien on the 99th Floor

Heinemann 1996

Fred is fed-up. He doesn't want to go shopping with Mum and baby brother Harry – especially on a wet Saturday morning. But when Fred gets left behind in the lift and whizzes up to floor 99, he meets an unusual friend and has a day full of fun.

Delilah Alone

Mammoth 1997

When Delilah's owner, Edward, goes abroad on holiday, Delilah cannot understand why she, the most beautiful and pampered cat of all, has been left alone. Feeling unloved and abandoned, Delilah sets off on an adventure away from her country home and into the grim life of the city.

Hot Dog Cool Cat

Mammoth 1997

Dennis is big and strong, likes rough-and-tumble games and calls himself Hot Dog. Claude is clever and elegant, a tom-about-town and calls himself Cool Cat. Since their owners want, respectively, a small fluffy gentle dog and a lovable lazy tabby, Hot Dog and Cool Cat have a brilliant idea – a swop!

Seth and the Strangers

Mammoth 1997

A dark cloud rains tiny whirling shapes on to the hills of Yorkshire. Seth knows that each spinning silver disc carries something no one on Earth has encountered before.

The Dragon's Child

Hodder 1997 (hb); 1998 (pb)

Dando the dragon is abandoned by his family when they fly off to the south and must somehow survive alone. An orphaned slave girl offers him hope because she knows he is a magical creature and their friendship keeps them safe, but for how long?

The Owl Tree

Walker 1997

An enormous leafy tree sometimes seems to speak like a person. Granny Diamond once saw an owl in the tree, but her neighbour, Mr Rock, wants to cut it down. Why does he dislike the owl tree so much?

Smarties Book Prize Gold Award 1997.

The Rinaldi Ring

Mammoth 1999

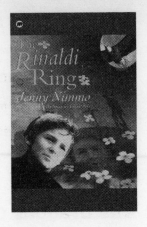

Eliot, grieving for his dead mother, is sent to stay with his cousins. There he is haunted by Mary-Ellen, who was once kept prisoner in his room. The loss of her fiancé, Orlando Rinaldi, killed in World War I threatened her sanity, or so everyone thought. Drawn to her story, Eliot has to right a terrible wrong.

Toby in the Dark

Walker 1999

Toby, a toy panda, has been hidden away in a dark loft for over sixty-five years. When the bullying, child-hating Mrs Malevant arrives, Toby wakes up and works to restore happiness to the troubled house.

Dog Star

Walker 1999

Marty's family won't let her have a dog, but one frosty night the dog star shines into her window and something flies across the room. It hides under Marty's bed. It's a dog. But is it real? And where has it really come from?

Ill Will, Well Nell

Egmont 2000

Will falls out of trees, crashes his bike and gets into all kinds of scrapes. Nell keeps herself tidy and is full of sensible advice. But together they have lots of fun, tussling over a tree-house and escaping from angry goats!

Tom and the Pterosaur

Walker 2001

Tom, the only boy in a family of girl singers, finds a strange creature in the barn next door. He and his sisters decide to set it free.

Milo's Wolves

Egmont 2001

Laura and Andy suddenly discover they have a brother, Gwendal. Laura knows the green lights in her father Milo's eyes mean there's more to the story than they've yet heard. As menacing figures from the sinister Society of Angels begin to circle the family, Gwendal's secret nature as a clone will put the whole family in danger.

Shortlisted for the Sheffield Book Award; selected by the DFES as a guided read for classes as an exemplar of work.

Something Wonderful

HarperCollins 2001

A small, unremarkable chicken proves that she can do something wonderful.

The Bodigulpa

Macmillan 2001

Something almost too gruesome to imagine happens in

Danny's greenhouse. What has his evil grandpa been growing in there?

Beak and Whisker

Egmont 2002

Tansy doesn't like birds, and she doesn't think much of boys either. So moving into a house with a roof full of squawking jackdaws, next door to a boy called Matthew, isn't her idea of fun. But Tansy and Matthew have to  rescue a baby jackdaw called Beak, and Tansy finds she might be brave enough to change her mind.

Midnight for Charlie Bone
Children of the Red King - Volume 1

Egmont 2002

Charlie Bone has a strange gift of being able to hear people talking in photographs. His Yewbeam relatives pack him off to Bloor's Academy, a school for geniuses and endowed children with similarly unusual gifts, where the headmaster and head boy, Dr Bloor and his son Manfred, can keep a close eye on him. Charlie finds himself in the middle of a war amongst the endowed, the

Children of the Red King, between those who work for good and those who want only evil.

The Night of the Unicorn

Walker 2003

A strange white horse appears in Mr Grace's animal sanctuary. The horse will have a profound effect on the lives of a lonely boy and two elderly chickens.

The Time Twister
Children of the Red King - Volume II

Egmont 2003

Henry Yewbeam has gazed into the depths of a dazzling marble, which twists him through time to meet Charlie

Bone, back for a new term at Bloor's Academy. Manfred's great-grandfather, Ezekiel Bloor, is Henry's cousin and tricked him with the Time Twister in 1916, when they were both children. Now, as an old man, Ezekiel still wants to create misery. Charlie must help Henry, ninety years out of his own time and still eleven years old, find a way out of Bloor's and away from the clutches of old Ezekiel.

The Time Twister

Chapter 1 - A Game of Marbles

It was January. 1916. The coldest winter in living memory.

The dark rooms in Bloor's Academy were almost as cold as the streets outside. Henry Yewbeam, hurrying down one of the icy passages, began to hum to himself. The humming cheered him up. It warmed his spirits as well as his feet.

On either side of the passage the eerie blue flames of gaslights flickered and hissed in their iron brackets. The smell was horrible. Henry wouldn't have been surprised to find something dead in one of the dark corners.

At home, in a sunny house by the sea, his sister, Daphne, was very ill with diphtheria. To avoid infection

Henry and his brother, James, had been sent to stay with their mother's brother, Sir Gideon Bloor.

Sir Gideon wasn't the sort of person you would choose to spend your holidays with. There was nothing remotely fatherly about him. He was the headmaster of an ancient school and he never let anyone forget it.

Bloor's Academy had been in Sir Gideon's family for hundreds of years. It was a school for children gifted in music, drama and art. Bloor's also took children who were endowed in other, very strange, ways. Just thinking about them made Henry shudder.

He had reached his cousin Zeke's room. Zeke was Sir Gideon's only child and a more unpleasant cousin Henry couldn't imagine. Zeke was one of the endowed children, but Henry guessed that Zeke's gift was probably nasty.

Henry opened the door and peeped inside. A row of glass jars stood on the windowsill. Inside the jars, strange things writhed gently in a clear liquid. Henry was sure it couldn't be water. The things were pale and shapeless. One was blue.

'What do you think you are doing?'

Aunt Gudrun came marching down the passage, her

long black skirt drowning her footfalls with a sinister hiss. She was a very tall woman with a great amount of yellow hair piled into a bun on the back of her head. A real Viking of a person (she was, in fact, Norwegian), with an enormous chest and lungs to match.

Henry said, 'Erm . . .'

'Erm is not good enough, Henry Yewbeam. You were spying in my Zeke's room, were you not?'

'No, not at all,' said Henry.

'You shouldn't be lurking in passages, boy. Come down to the sitting room.' Lady Bloor beckoned with her little finger, and Henry had no choice but to follow her.

His aunt led him back past the mysterious locked doors that, only a few moments ago, Henry had been vainly trying to open. He was an inquisitive boy and easily bored. A huge sigh escaped him as he trundled down a creaking staircase to the first floor.

The Bloor family lived in the west wing of the academy, but they only occupied the rooms above the ground floor, which was almost entirely taken up by a draughty grand hall, a chapel and several assembly halls and classrooms. Henry had already explored some of these rooms and found them very disappointing. All they contained were rows of battered desks and chairs, and shelves of dusty-looking books.

'Here we are!' Lady Bloor opened a door and thrust Henry into the room beyond.

A small boy, who had been kneeling in the window seat, leapt down and rushed across to Henry. 'Where've you been?' he cried.

'Just exploring,' said Henry.

'I thought you'd gone home.'

'Home is miles and miles away, Jamie.' Henry plonked himself in a deep leather chair beside the fire. The logs in the big iron grate smouldered with strange images. When Henry half-closed his eyes he could almost see the cosy sitting-room at home. He sighed again.

Aunt Gudrun frowned at Henry and said, 'Behave yourselves, boys.' She went out closing the door behind her.

When she had gone James came and sat on the arm of Henry's chair. 'Zeke's been doing funny things,' he whispered.

Henry hadn't noticed Zeke, but now he became

aware of his strange cousin, enclosed in a gloomy silence at the other end of the room. He was sitting at a table, absorbed in something laid out before him. His pale, bony face was frozen in an attitude of intense concentration. Not a muscle twitched, not a breath escaped him.

'I was scared,' James said quietly.

'Why? What did he do?' Henry asked in a hushed voice.

'Well, he was doing a puzzle. There were pieces all over the table. Then Zeke stared at them and they all crawled together. Well, most of them. They made a picture. He showed it to me. It was a ship, but some of the pieces wouldn't fit.'

'It's rude to whisper,' said Zeke without taking his eyes off the puzzle.

Henry pulled himself out of the chair and strolled over to his cousin. He glanced at the twelve pieces lying beside the puzzle and then at the picture of the ship. It took less than a minute for him to see exactly where each piece fitted.

'Hm,' said Henry, and without another word he picked up the single pieces, one by one, and deftly placed them into the picture; two in the sky, three in the ship's hull, two in the rigging and four in the sea.

For a moment, Zeke watched Henry's hands in fascination. It was only when Henry was putting the last piece in place, that Zeke suddenly leapt up, crying, 'Who asked you? I could have done it. I could!'

'Sorry,' said Henry, stepping back. 'I thought you wanted some help.'

'Henry's good at puzzles,' said James.

'Well I'm good at *other* things,' snarled Zeke.

James was too small to see the danger signs. The angry glitter in Zeke's black eyes went straight over his head. 'Magic doesn't always work,' the little boy said blithely. 'Henry's cleverer than you are, Zeke.'

With that remark poor James Yewbeam sealed his brother's fate and, of course, his own.

'Get out!' cried Zeke. 'Both of you. Hateful Yewbeams. Go, now. I can't stand the sight of you!'

Henry and James ran for the door. There was a violent gleam in their cousin's pale face, and they didn't want to wait around for him to do something nasty.

'Where are we going?' panted James as he tore down the passages after his brother.

'We'll go to the big hall, Jamie. We can play marbles there.' Henry pulled a small leather bag out of his pocket and waved it at his brother.

It wasn't to be. Before they could go any further there was a shout from Aunt Gudrun.

'James, bedtime.' James pretended not to hear her. 'Now, this minute.'

'Better go,' said Henry gently. 'She'll punish you, if you don't.'

'But I want to play marbles,' said James.

Henry shook his head. 'Sorry, Jamie. Not now. Tomorrow. But I'll come and read to you later.'

'Promise? Will you finish the story of the Wallypug?'

'James, come here,' shouted Aunt Gudrun.

'I promise,' said Henry, and he meant to keep his promise. But Zeke had other plans for him.

Hanging his head, James trailed back towards the tall figure at the end of the passage.

'And you, Henry!' called Aunt Gudrun. 'You keep out of trouble.'

'Yes, Aunt,' said Henry.

He was about to descend the rather grand staircase down to the hall when he had an idea. It was already so chilly he could see his own breath, billowing away from him in little grey clouds. The great hall would be even colder. He might freeze to death.

Henry retraced his steps until he found the door to a room he had already investigated. It was a huge storeroom, full of clothes left behind by past students of the academy. There were rows of coloured capes: blue, green and purple; shelves of hats and suits, and boxes of ancient leather boots.

Henry selected a warm blue cape and put it on. It reached well over his knees, a perfect length for a draughty hall. He would be able to kneel on it without feeling the cold stone floor.

Henry descended into the hall. His hoard of marbles was the envy of all his friends. Henry's father travelled extensively and never came home without at least one precious new marble for his son's collection. Henry's leather bag held onyx stones, polished agate, glass, limestone, quartz and even spheres of painted china.

There were no lights in the hall but an early moon sparkled through the long, frosted windows, giving the grey flagstones a soft pearly glow.

Henry decided to play Ring Taw, his favourite game.

Deprived of an opponent, he would try to improve his skill by playing alone. With a piece of chalk, kept handy in his pocket, Henry drew a large ring in the centre of the hall. He then chalked a smaller ring inside the first. Selecting thirteen marbles from his bag, he placed them in a cross inside the smaller circle.

Now Henry had to kneel on the icy floor, just outside the large ring. Already his hands were blue with cold and he could hardly stop his teeth from rattling. Tucking the blue cape under his knees, he took out his favourite marble; it was a clear blue with a silvery glint inside it, like starlight. This was always his taw, or shooter.

Placing the knuckles of his right hand, palm outwards, on the floor, Henry put the blue taw on the tip of his first finger and flicked it with his thumb towards the marble cross. With a sharp clink it hit an orange marble right out of the two circles.

'Bravo!' Henry shouted.

There was a light creak from behind him. Henry squinted into the deep shadows on the oak-panelled walls. Was he imagining it, or did a long tapestry shiver slightly? On the other side of the tapestry a small door led into the west wing. Henry preferred the main staircase, for the passage behind the door was dark and creepy.

A cold draught swept past his knees and the tapestry billowed again. A flurry of hailstones clattered against the windows, and the wind gave a sudden moan as it rushed round the snowy courtyard.

'Wind.' Henry shivered and drew his cape closer. For good measure he even pulled the hood over his head.

In the passage behind the tapestry, Ezekiel Bloor stood with a lantern in one hand, and in the other – a glowing glass sphere. Dazzling colours swirled out of the glass; a rainbow laced with gold and silver; sunshine and moonlight, one after the other. Zeke knew he mustn't look at them. He held one of the oldest marbles in the world.

On her deathbed, Zeke's great-aunt Beatrice, a witch if ever there was one, had pressed the marble into his hand. 'The Time Twister,' she said in her cracked, dying voice. 'For journeys through time. Do not look on it, Ezekiel, unless you want to travel.'

Ezekiel didn't want to travel. He thrived in the great gloomy building that was his home and could seldom be persuaded to leave it. However, he longed to know what would happen if someone *did* look into the Time Twister. No one, in Zeke's opinion, was more deserving of a shove through time, than his wretched cousin Henry Yewbeam.

Henry had by now knocked another three marbles out of the small chalked ring. He hadn't missed once, in spite of his freezing fingers. He was just stepping back to his place outside the circle when a glass ball came rolling towards him. It was slightly larger than Henry's blue taw, and tiny points of coloured light danced and shimmered all around it.

'Oh, my,' breathed Henry. He stood where he was while the strange marble rolled on until it reached his foot.

Henry picked it up. He gazed into the bright depths within the glass. He saw domes of gold, cities in sunlight, cloudless skies and much, much more. But even as he watched the scenes taking place before his eyes, Henry became aware that a change was taking place within his body, and he knew that he shouldn't have looked upon those unbelievable and breathtaking scenes.

The oak-panelled walls were breaking up. The

frosted moonlight was fading. Henry's head whirled and his feet began to float. Far, far away, a cat began to mew. And then another cat, and another.

Henry thought of his small brother. Would there be time to reach him before he faded away completely? And if he did, and James saw a brother disappearing before his eyes, might he not be so frightened he would have nightmares forever? Henry decided to leave a message.

While he still had the strength, he took the chalk from his pocket and with his left hand (the right was still clamped round the Time Twister), he wrote on the stone floor, 'SORRY, JAMES. THE MARBLES . . .'

It was all Henry had time for. The next moment he had left the year of his eleventh birthday and was travelling forward, very fast, to a year when most of the people he knew would be dead.

In a small, chilly room at the top of the west wing, James waited for his brother. He was so cold he had put his coat on over his flannel nightshirt. On the table beside him the flame from his candle, quivered in a draught from the door. Where was Henry? Why was he taking so long?

James rubbed his eyes. He was very tired but too cold to sleep. He drew the bedcovers up to his chin and listened to the patter of freezing sleet against the windowpane. And then his candle went out.

James sat rigid in his bed, too frightened to call out. Aunt Gudrun would be cross and Cousin Zeke would tease him for being a baby. Only Henry would understand.

'Henry! Henry, where are you?' James closed his eyes and sobbed into his pillow.

Before he had completely run out of tears, James stopped shivering. The room was getting warmer. He opened his eyes and found that he could see his pillow, his hand, the window. A soft glow had spread across the ceiling. When James looked to see where it was coming from, he was amazed to find that three cats were silently pacing round his bed. One was orange, another yellow and the third a bright coppery colour.

As soon as the cats knew they had been observed, they jumped up and rubbed their heads against the boy's cold hands, his neck and his cheek. Their gleaming fur was as warm as sunlight, and as James stroked them, his fear began to leave him. He decided to go and look for Henry. Hardly had this thought entered his head than the cats leapt off the bed and ran to the door. They waited, mewing anxiously, as James pulled on his socks and his small leather boots.

With light sparkling on their silver whiskers and bright fur-tips, the cats led the way down the dark passages and narrow steps, while James hurried after them. At last he came to the wide staircase leading down into the hall. Here the cats' worried mewing became loud and urgent, and James hesitated before he descended into the vast moonlit room.

Henry was not there. His marbles lay scattered on the stone floor, winking in the bright frosted light from the windows. As James moved slowly down the stairs, the cats ran before him, wailing and growling.

James reached the bottom step and walked to the chalked circle. He could see that Henry had been playing Ring Taw, his favourite game.

'Henry!' James called. 'Henry, where have you gone?'

Never had a place appeared so vast and empty to small James Yewbeam. Never had his brother's absence seemed so utterly complete. He wouldn't try to call again. It was quite clear that Henry was gone. And he hadn't even said goodbye.

Before the tears could fall again, the three cats pounced into the white circle, drawing the boy's attention to four words chalked on the floor. A message? If only James could read. Henry had been patiently trying to teach him for weeks but, so far, James hadn't managed a single word.

Perhaps he hadn't really tried. Now, when it was a serious matter . . .

'S . . . s . . . s . . .' murmured James as the cats paced along the row of letters.

Next came an 'o' and then two 'r's, and further on his own name. And all at once James found he could understand the words his brother had left for him.

'SORRY, JAMES,' he read, 'THE MARBLES . . .' There the message ended.

Obviously Henry wanted his brother to keep the marbles safe for him. James picked up the leather bag but before he could reach the blue taw, the orange cat tapped it playfully and it sped across the hall. The yellow cat raced after it while the copper cat swept another three marbles out of the ring.

Now the great hall was alive with the sound of clinking glass and joyful purring. James was surrounded by dancing, glistening spheres of colour. The cats were playing a game and, as he watched them, a big smile broke over the boy's face.

'Stay with me,' James begged the cats.

The cats would stay. For as long as he was in that cold, dreary building, they would keep James Yewbeam as warm and safe as any small boy had a right to expect.

Other authors in the series

An interview with

J.K. Rowling

Creator of the bestselling
Harry Potter

An interview with

Anne Fine

The award-winning author
and children's laureate

An interview with

Jacqueline Wilson

The best-selling author
of The Illustrated Mum

An interview with

Jamila Gavin

The best-selling author of Coram Boy

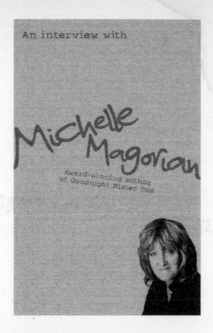

An interview with

Michelle Magorian

Award-winning author
of Goodnight Mister Tom

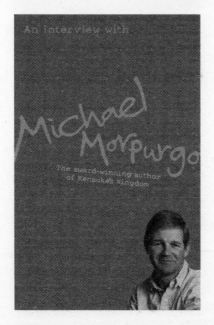

An interview with

Michael Morpurgo

The award-winning author
of Kensuke's Kingdom